WITHDRAWN

J362.18
P   Peltak
              Call to rescue, call
          to heal

United We Stand
AMERICA RESPONDS TO THE EVENTS OF September 11, 2001

CALL TO RESCUE, CALL TO HEAL
Emergency Medical Professionals at Ground Zero

FIRST TO ARRIVE
Firefighters at Ground Zero

GUARDIANS OF SAFETY
Law Enforcement at Ground Zero

HELPING HANDS
A City and a Nation Lend Their Support at Ground Zero

KEEPING THE PEACE
The U.S. Military Responds to Terror

WE THE PEOPLE
The U.S. Government's United Response Against Terror

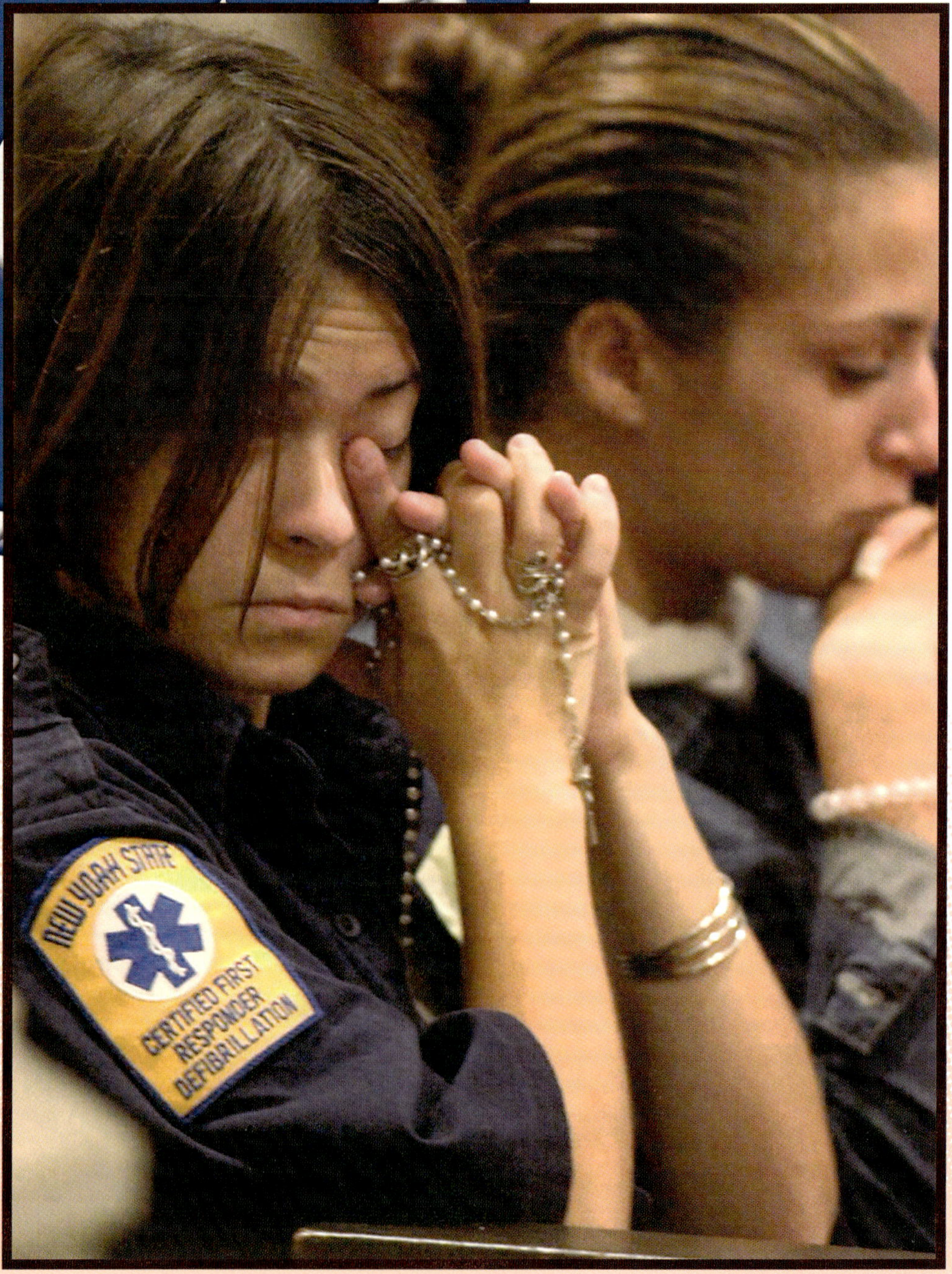
NEW YORK STATE
CERTIFIED FIRST RESPONDER DEFIBRILLATION

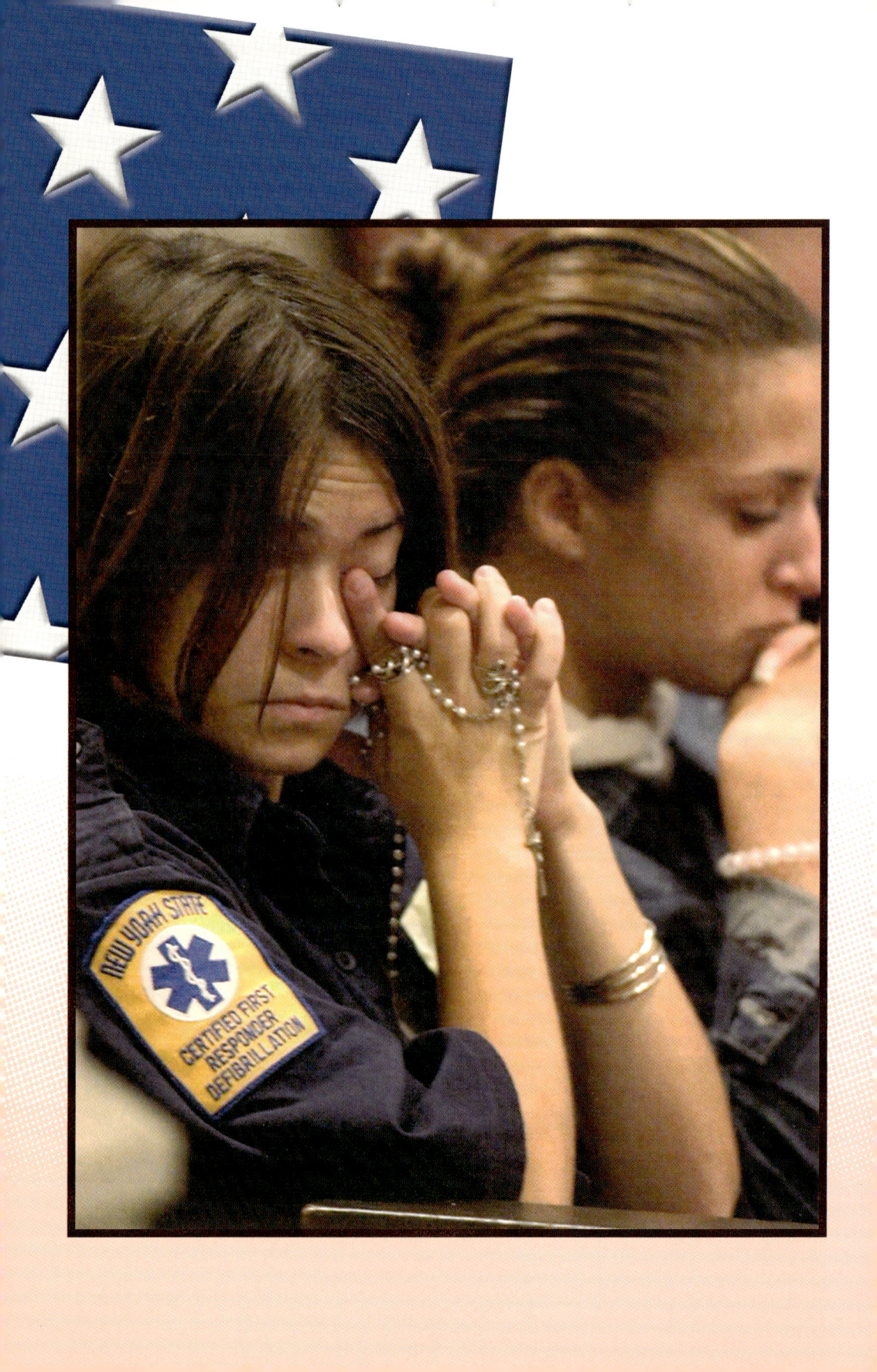

United We Stand
AMERICA RESPONDS TO THE EVENTS OF
September 11, 2001

CALL TO RESCUE, CALL TO HEAL

Emergency Medical Professionals at Ground Zero

Jennifer Peltak

CHELSEA HOUSE PUBLISHERS
A Haights Cross Communications Company

PHILADELPHIA

FRONTIS: An EMT wipes away tears at a mass held at St. Patrick's Cathedral in New York honoring uniformed men and women killed on September 11.

CHELSEA HOUSE PUBLISHERS

EDITOR IN CHIEF Sally Cheney
DIRECTOR OF PRODUCTION Kim Shinners
CREATIVE MANAGER Takeshi Takahashi
MANUFACTURING MANAGER Diann Grasse

STAFF FOR CALL TO RESCUE, CALL TO HEAL

ASSOCIATE EDITOR Benjamin Xavier Kim
PICTURE RESEARCHER Sarah Bloom
PRODUCTION ASSISTANT Jaimie Winkler
COVER AND SERIES DESIGNER Keith Trego
LAYOUT 21st Century Publishing and Communications, Inc.

©2003 by Chelsea House Publishers,
a subsidiary of Haights Cross Communications.
All rights reserved. Printed and bound in the United States of America.

A Haights Cross Communications Company

http://www.chelseahouse.com

First Printing

1 3 5 7 9 8 6 4 2

Library of Congress Cataloging-in-Publication Data

Peltak, Jennifer.
   Call to rescue, call to heal : emergency medical professionals at ground zero / Jennifer Peltak.
      p. cm.—(United we stand)
Includes index.
   ISBN 0-7910-7180-4
   1. Emergency medical services—New York (State)—New York.
2. Emergency medical services—Virginia—Arlington. 3. Emergency medical technicians. 4. September 11 Terrorist Attacks, 2001.
I. Title. II. Series.
RA645.6.N7 P45 2002
362.18'0973—dc21
                                                                2002006999

TABLE OF CONTENTS

FOREWORD by Benjamin Xavier Kim — 6

A COMMITMENT TO CARING — 9

THE EVOLUTION OF EMERGENCY CARE — 19

THE GOLDEN HOUR AND BEYOND — 33

JUST PART OF THE JOB — 41

SERVING THROUGH DISASTER — 47

LIFE AFTER SEPTEMBER 11 — 53

WEBSITES — 60
AGENCIES — 60
FURTHER READING — 60
BIBLIOGRAPHY — 61
INDEX — 64

Foreword

The events of September 11, 2001 will be remembered as one of the most devastating attacks on American soil ever. The terrorist attacks caused not only physical destruction but also shattered America's sense of safety and security, and highlighted the fact that there were many groups in the world that did not embrace the United States and its far-reaching influence. While things have, for the most part, returned to normal, there is still no escaping the demarcation of life before and after September 11—the newest day that will forever live in infamy.

Yet, even in the aftermath of the terror and destruction, one can see some positive effects that have arisen from the attacks. Americans' interest in foreign countries—especially those where Islam is the predominant religion—and U.S. foreign policy has been at an all-time high. The previously mundane occupations of firefighter, police officer and emergency medical worker have taken on a newfound level of respect due to the heroism and selflessness displayed on September 11. The issue of airport security has finally been taken seriously with

FOREWORD

the implementation of National Guardsmen in airports and undercover air marshals aboard flights.

The books in this series describe how various groups and agencies dealt with the unfolding events of September 11. They also tell the history of these agencies and how they have dealt with other crises in the past, as well as how they are operating in the wake of September 11.

While the rest of us were reeling in shock and horror at what was unfolding before our eyes, there were others whose jobs required that they confront the situation head-on. These are their stories.

Benjamin Xavier Kim
Series Editor

When terrorists flew hijacked planes into the towers of the World Trade Center and into the Pentagon, there was no time for EMTs to waste. Despite the overwhelming shock of the events that had occurred, they had to make sure to attend to the injured and prevent the tragedy from spiraling out of control.

1

A Commitment to Caring

EMTs and Paramedics on September 11

"We have just witnessed an aircraft hit the World Trade Center." The words of emergency medical technician Alex Loutsky flashed across the screen of an emergency dispatcher in Brooklyn. The 911 call came just after 8:47 A.M. on the bright, Indian summer morning of September 11. Loutsky and his partner, Eric Ramos, were sitting in their ambulance near the World Trade Center when they witnessed the unthinkable: an airplane had slammed into the North Tower.

"I said, 'Eric, hold on a second, look at that plane! That plane is too low! It's going to hit something!' And then I go . . . 'It's going to hit! It's going to hit!' And, 'Bam! Boom! Explosion,'" Loutsky recalled.

The 12-year EMT veteran from Staten Island trembled as he reported the deadly crash of Flight 11. "Every cell in my body just seized. It's just like I quivered and I knew I had basically one chance to get it right on the radio, so I couldn't, like, get emotional or anything. I had to say it correctly. It was the most chilling moment of my life."

The fire department dispatcher initially logged the call as "BLDG Explosion." Less than a minute later, at 8:48 A.M., the incident was updated to "Explosion On Top of World Trade." Four seconds later, horror became history: "Plane Into Top of BLDG."

Loutsky and Ramos were the first emergency team to report the attack, and theirs was the first Fire Department ambulance at the World Trade Center. Shortly after their fateful call, ambulances began arriving at the smoking north tower. At 8:50, the Brooklyn dispatcher recorded the arrival of EMTs Mario Santoro and Keith Fairben.

At the eastern edge of the Trade Center, Loutsky and Ramos set up a makeshift triage station to help the injured and frightened workers who had begun fleeing from the tower. Triage stations, a critical facility in mass casualty situations, are essentially makeshift emergency rooms set up near the scene of an incident. There, EMTs and other medical professionals can examine the injured and prioritize who receives treatment first. "We basically had to choose among many victims where they would go and who would go, depending on the severity of their injuries," Loutsky said.

By 8:59, two more EMTs—Yamel Merino and Carlos Lillo—arrived at the towers. Merino, a 24-year-old single mother, stopped to say a prayer before she joined her fellow EMTs and paramedics at a triage center. Lillo arrived with a friend from high school, Moussa Diaz, a fellow EMT. They had just delivered a pregnant woman to a hospital in Queens when news of the crash screamed through their radios: "A plane hit the twin towers!" Sirens wailing, they sped to Manhattan. As they came into view of the blazing trade center, it struck Diaz that the North Tower looked like a "lit cigarette standing on its filter end."

Triage centers and temporary staging areas were hastily set up around the World Trade Center perimeter. Diaz reported first to a

A Commitment to Caring

temporary command post to receive his instructions. As he approached, bloody and burned people swarmed around him. The first woman he treated suffered from third-degree burns. Her shock was so great she couldn't feel the skin peeling off her face. Diaz took the woman to the St. Vincent's Hospital emergency room and raced back. It was 9:03.

Four minutes later, a terrifying new message broke across the fire department dispatcher screen: "Second Plane Hit the Second Building." Flight 175 had ripped through the south tower. The two towers boiled over with fire and the sky darkened from smoke and debris. People trapped on floors above the crash points began leaping from windows, desperate to escape the heat and smoke.

On the ground, hundreds of police officers, firefighters, EMTs and paramedics rushed into the World Trade Center to rescue the injured and direct terrified workers out of the buildings. Outside the towers, paramedics lined up stretchers around the buildings and scores of emergency medical teams packed people into ambulances. "We would open the door and they would pour in," said paramedic Lisandro Rijos, a member of the third unit on the scene. "We'd have 10 people in the back, and we're only supposed to have four." Though no one knew yet how badly the towers were damaged, EMTs and paramedics were rushing as many people as possible away from

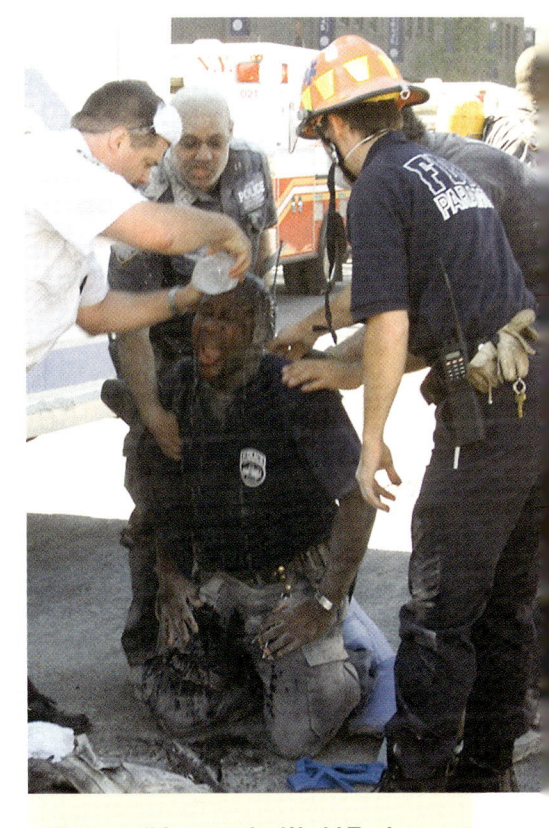

The conditions at the World Trade Center were not only difficult to deal with but hazardous as well, requiring emergency workers to take breaks and receive assistance themselves before continuing their work.

the scene. "We'd close the [ambulance door] and just say go, go, go!" recalled Rijos.

Moussa Diaz was tending to an elderly woman whose heart was clenching after walking down 87 flights of stairs when he heard the voice of his friend, Carlos Lillo, over the radio. "I'm going in! I'm going in to get my wife." Lillo's pregnant wife, Cecilia, worked on the 64th floor of the North Tower. Other paramedics urged Lillo to stay put, saying that Cecilia would find her way out, but the EMT disappeared into the building.

As EMTs, paramedics, and other rescue workers at the World Trade Center struggled to contain the pandemonium erupting around them, at 9:43 A.M., Flight 77 plunged into the Pentagon in Arlington, Virginia. As fire raged through a smoking crater in the Pentagon's side, employees raced from the military complex. EMTs and paramedics were among the first to arrive at the scene. A local fire and emergency medical services (EMS) captain recalled that despite the confusion, responding emergency workers set up a triage center almost immediately. "I set up triage, treatment and transport sectors in a grassy area on a hill with a good vantage point of the incident. I special ordered 20 paramedic units and a bus for the walking wounded, along with a couple of helicopters," Ed Blunt told the *Journal of Emergency Medical Services*. "We weren't alone on the scene. There was an outpouring of help from

"You could hear the alarms of the firefighters' airpacks, signaling they were out of air, you could hear moaning and you couldn't get in to help. We pointed people in the right direction; they were running into walls, hurt, people lying there with broken legs, hundreds of people. We had to drag or carry them. . . . I stepped on an amputated leg. . . . I taped up my knee. We were giving oxygen and bandages, using their clothing to stop the bleeding . . . just one loss is too much."

Kenneth Davis, paramedic

A Commitment to Caring

Emergency personnel at Pentagon assess the situation at hand before taking action.

military personnel—doctors, nurses, paramedics, EMTs, stretcher-bearers." Blunt was tending to burn victims when everyone was ordered to evacuate because of reports of another plane headed toward Washington, D.C. "We all agreed we weren't going to leave those patients," Blunt said. Instead, Blunt and his fellow emergency workers quickly loaded the patients into ambulances and a helicopter and ordered them to the nearest hospital.

EMTs and paramedics on the scene "laid mats on the grass for the wounded, set up intravenous lines, and organized teams of litter-bearers," according to one report. Others ran into the building bearing stretchers. Ambulances from neighboring counties joined in the rescue effort. Stations left vacant by rescue workers responding to the Pentagon were filled with EMTs and paramedics from outer counties. Volunteer EMTs who worked inside the Pentagon aided victims for as long as they could stand the choking smoke and heat.

Nearly a half-hour after the attack on the Pentagon, Flight 93 crashed in a field in Pennsylvania. EMTs and paramedics arrived at the crash site within minutes, but there were no survivors.

While the first terrifying minutes after the crash at the Pentagon unfolded, the situation at the World Trade Center was worsening.

Dispatchers recorded calls from people reporting that floors were collapsing underneath them. Triage centers sprouted up around the World Trade Center but rescue workers were continually pushed back as dangerous debris fell around them. EMTs and paramedics worked quickly but calmly to bandage, splint and stabilize the injured and direct the uninjured to safety. "We pointed people in the right direction; they were running into walls, hurt, people lying there with broken legs, hundreds of people. We had to drag them or carry them," said Kenneth Davis, a paramedic at the World Trade Center. "We told them to go down the block and don't stop . . . We were giving oxygen and bandages, using their clothing to stop the bleeding." One EMT estimated that he loaded at least 50 injured people into ambulances. Another EMT at the scene, Keith Fairben, received a call from his father, a volunteer firefighter, warning him about the plane crashes. "Dad," the 24-year-old replied, "I'm really busy. I'm at the World Trade Center. I can't talk now."

EMTs and paramedics flowed in from around the city to help. Brian Smith and Brian Gordon, partners and brand-new EMTs, responded to a report of injured people waiting near the trade center in the Engine Company 10/Ladder Company 10 firehouse. They arrived at the station with mass-casualty incident wrist tags: green and yellow for the injured; red for those needing urgent help; and black for those beyond help. The two tagged the injured, sending them off with police officers, and put a brace on one man with a fractured hip. After they heard the impact of the second plane, Gordon and Smith prepared the firehouse by setting up chairs and arranging blankets and pillows for the scores of wounded people they were expecting. Smith was loading Snapples into a truck for firefighters when he heard an ominous, deafening rumble.

Minutes after 10 A.M., the rumbling turned into a roar. The south tower was collapsing. Moussa Diaz looked up from his elderly patient to see the fearsome black cloud of snapped steel, glass, ash, body parts and other debris rushing toward them. "Run!" he screamed at the woman. Another EMT was setting up

A Commitment to Caring

a triage center a few blocks away when the tower fell. "Afterwards we had no equipment, no vehicles . . . Ten minutes straight of blackness." Even in darkness, rescue workers tried to help. One paramedic described the first women he helped as crawling toward him on all fours, coughing. Later, the search for more people turned gruesome. He discovered more body parts than bodies. At Fire Station 10, the fierce force of the blast threw Smith against a concrete wall and trapped Gordon beneath a pile of people. After seemingly endless minutes, the dust settled and they were able to radio for help. Gordon sprained his ankle and shoulder and Smith suffered from a concussion, but duty and training asserted itself. They were tending to survivors when a fire company responded to their call, and the two helped lift the injured through a kitchen window before they allowed themselves to be rescued.

Emergency workers carry a fellow worker from one of the World Trade Center's collapsing towers. The collapse of the buildings caught many workers under ash and rubble, and some did not survive.

While paramedics and EMTs at the World Trade Center contended with the paralyzing cloud of ash, paramedic Steven Craver had just deposited six patients, including one with a broken bone protruding from her wrist and another with third-degree burns, at a hospital. He stocked his ambulance with water, filter masks, sheets, and towels and headed back to the towers, just before 10:30. As he reached them, the north tower began its agonizing crumble. Craver packed his ambulance again and fled the scene before the mushroom cloud of debris reached him and his patients.

Call to Rescue, Call to Heal

As the towers fell, EMTs and paramedics joined the stampede of injured and endangered lives fleeing the calamity. Alex Loutsky and Eric Ramos were at their makeshift triage center during the second collapse. They escaped on foot as fire engulfed their ambulance. One paramedic, fleeing with a police officer, told the officer to shoot open the door of a locked building. The officer did, allowing the medic and scores of people into the safety of the building.

Many rescue workers who survived limped out of the cloud of black ash with broken and sprained limbs, concussions, cuts and bruises, burns, abrasions from flying glass, and respiratory injuries. The latex gloves of one EMT caught fire as he searched the ruined towers for trapped victims. He left his post only after suffering chest pains. Hospitals and nearby triage centers had braced themselves for an onslaught of victims. They treated mostly injured and exhausted police officers, firefighters, EMTs and paramedics.

Moussa Diaz was chased from the World Trade Center once more after the second tower collapsed. After fleeing several blocks to Lafayette Square, he returned to treat people, even though his damaged lungs made breathing difficult. Brian Smith and Brian Gordon carried a man with a broken pelvis several blocks and waited with him until a police car arrived. Gordon could barely walk and Smith's neck was swollen with whiplash, but when they were later assigned to a woman suffering from an anxiety attack, they comforted her for an hour.

Hundreds of rescue workers perished when the twin towers collapsed. Dispatchers reported the crackle of radios from firefighters and EMTs trapped in the debris. One medic, sent to relieve other rescuers, died after a walkway collapsed. Yamel Merino, who had reported to the World Trade Center shortly after the first plane hit, hadn't been seen since. Keith Fairben's father called a dispatcher that first night and discovered his son was missing. Carlos Lillo's wife had safely made it out of the South Tower but her husband had not been seen since he went to rescue her. Brian Smith's father, a firefighter, had last been seen on the 11th floor of South Tower.

Volunteer EMTs and paramedics who were not assigned to duty

A Commitment to Caring

that day rushed to the World Trade Center, driven by a commitment to helping others. Some paid with their lives. One 23-year-old EMT never reported to his job at a medical institute on September 11. His family assumes he went to the World Trade Center when he learned of the attack. A Virginia man and volunteer EMT who had been on a business trip three blocks away from the World Trade Center was also missing. "The only thing I can think of is he went to help," his wife said.

Paramedics embrace on September 13, 2001 and recount their own experiences of September 11. For paramedics, the tragedy of fallen comrades coupled with the horror of the event brought them even closer together.

Eight New York City EMTs and paramedics died September 11: Keith Fairben, Carlos Lillo, Yamel Merino, Richard Pearlman, Ricardo Quinn, Mark Schwartz, Mario Santoro, and David Marc Sullins. Despite the devastating loss of life, the New York paramedics union estimates that 2,500 people were taken by ambulance from the World Trade Center.

When the scope of the tragedy became apparent, the federal government dispatched federal disaster emergency teams from as far away as Oklahoma to assist at Ground Zero and the Pentagon. Each 35-member team consisted of doctors, nurses, and EMTs equipped to treat trauma victims and perform triage. It wasn't just those EMTs and medics called to duty who helped. As darkness fell on New York City that Tuesday night, one former EMT, a tourist visiting from Arizona, joined the scores of volunteers assisting the rescue effort.

"I think they're going to need all the help they can get," she said.

A dispatcher at a 911 emergency center. Although we may take 911 for granted today, the number '911' itself was not designated as the universal emergency number until 1968.

2

The Evolution of Emergency Care

From Ambulance Attendants to Paramedics

Summoning help to the scene of a car accident or for someone who is suffering a heart attack is as easy as dialing 911. Trained professionals or volunteers known as emergency medical technicians (EMTs) and paramedics (an EMT with the highest level of training) are quickly dispatched to the injured and the ill to provide vital emergency care while transporting patients to the nearest hospital. The EMT and paramedic are trained to deal with shortness of breath, heart attacks, gunshot wounds, burns, cuts, electric shocks, stabbings, broken bones, and any other injury or illness that can befall a human being. In the past 40 years, the public has come to recognize that immediate treatment for an accident or illness is often a necessity for survival and recovery. From dense urban neighborhoods to remote mountain communities, a volunteer or professional squad of EMTs and paramedics now serve nearly every corner of the United States. The speed, ability, and dedication of these men and women are major reasons why the majority of Americans call on EMTs and paramedics during medical emergencies. In New York City, for instance, the fire department's Emergency Medical Service (EMS) units responded to over a million medical emergencies in 2000.

Everyday EMTs and paramedics are expected to make perfect, split-second decisions that can result in life or death for their patients. For that reason, training for EMTs and paramedic is rigorous, involving long classroom hours and extensive work in the field. Paramedics must complete a two-year, college-level program to be certified. There are federal guidelines that potential EMTs and paramedics must meet, and each state has its own set of requirements. Because of rapid advances in the field of medicine and the increasingly sophisticated equipment that EMTs and paramedics use, they must be recertified every two years. Ongoing training is simply a fact of the EMT and paramedic's life. Less than 40 years ago, however, the federal government had no guidelines for emergency medical care. 911 did not yet exist. Each community developed its own system to help the injured and sick.

In fact, the concept of emergency medical care only dates back to the 18th century. Its birthplace, not surprisingly, was the battlefield. Napoleon's chief surgeon, Baron Dominique Jean Larrey, saw that injured soldiers were left on the battlefield for as long as two weeks. This waste of life caused Larrey to "realize the importance of providing expeditious care for those injured in battled and [he] established the first organized triage and trauma system". His horse-drawn carriages, known as "The Flying Ambulances of Larrey," were one of the earliest attempts to move the wounded to a defined care setting where physicians were waiting. Treatment in the field did not yet exist but these early emergency rooms were located close to the battlefield to minimize travel time. The care was crude by today's standards. Nevertheless, the idea of bringing immediate service to the injured instead of transporting them to a hospital or their home had taken root.

Still, it would be a while before U.S. doctors followed suit. During the Civil War's Battle of Bull Run, many wounded soldiers were simply left to die on the battlefield. A report on the battlefield conditions was sent to President Lincoln, who fired his surgeon-general and appointed one who followed Napoleonic principles of immediate emergency care. However, emergency medical services for ordinary citizens did not appear until the 1860s when Cincinnati and New York City established the first civilian ambulance services. In an era of dirt roads and horse-drawn ambulances, these so-called "ambulance attendants" were not noted for their speedy service. In the early years of New York City's ambulance service, calls came in via telegraph from Bellevue Hospital. Any doctor present could be dispatched to the patient. If the call volume increased, though, anyone on duty at the hospital might be sent—including a janitor or member of the kitchen staff. The care might have appeared dubious at times, but the

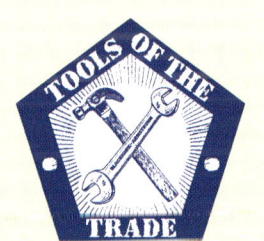

THE AMBULANCE

In the early 20th century, ambulances replaced horse-drawn carriages to transport the sick and ill. Ambulances are stocked with the basic tools and sophisticated machinery needed to stabilize a patient until they can reach the hospital. They are also expensive: the typical ambulance costs up to $150,000. Each ambulance contains a gurney, stretchers, backboards, neck collars, oxygen, endotrachael tubes, defibrillator, EKG, gloves, a variety of drugs, pillows and towels, syringes, child-sized equipment, splints, and bandages. Ambulances receive daily maintenance and supplies are restocked after each hospital run.

Call to Rescue, Call to Heal

An ambulance for Bellevue Hospital in New York, circa 1896. New York was one of the first cities in the US to establish ambulance services.

hospital responded to more than 1,800 calls in their first year of service. The crews sent out consisted of a driver and someone to care for the patient. Due to lack of technology and lengthy travel time, the more seriously injured patients usually died before they reached the hospital. Despite the drawbacks, providing emergency care was a growing necessity of the industrial age. The advent of cars and other heavy machinery meant more—and increasingly severe—accidents.

In rural areas, emergency care usually fell to the local police and fire departments, although the local undertaker often provided a hearse for transport. However, providing emergency support in addition to their regular duties taxed the resources of police and firefighters. Until Red Cross first aid training was introduced in the early 1900s, no one except a doctor could help an injured person at the scene of an accident. The dawn of the volunteer medic came in 1928, when the first-known independent volunteer rescue squad began operation in Roanoke, Virginia. Its founder, Julian Stanley Wise, witnessed two canoeists drown in the Roanoke

The Evolution of Emergency Care

River when he was a child, and he resolved afterward to become a lifesaver. After the Virginia squad formed, rescue squads soon followed in Texas and New Jersey. Wise went on to establish the International First Aid and Rescue Association in 1948.

By mid-century, medical personnel recognized the importance of emergency pre-hospital treatment. Still, most hospitals lacked a sophisticated system for rescuing the sick and injured. In New York City, ambulance personnel worked their regular duties until a call came in, which resulted in extended response times. The ambulance crew still consisted of a driver and doctor—neither of whom received training in the other's duties. Little was offered in the way of emergency medicine. These so-called "scoop and run" operations were further limited when the ambulance had to return to its base hospital, regardless of whether another hospital was closer to the scene of an accident.

While civilian ambulance services and volunteer rescue squads slowly evolved, emergency medical treatment was rapidly advancing on the field of the 20th century's numerous conflicts. The availability of penicillin greatly improved treatment during World War II. Medics in World War Two and, later, the Korean and Vietnam conflicts also developed lifesaving skills that they shared with hospitals when they returned home. During the Korean War, helicopters and jeeps came into use, greatly speeding patient evacuation and their chances of survival. Tools medics used on the battlefield, such as stretchers and plastic IV containers, were introduced to help civilian injuries. As training improved, protocols and rules to guide the ambulance attendants came into being. In the 1950s, the American College of Surgeons developed the first training program for ambulance attendants.

Emergency care was maturing but it was still highly fragmented, dependent entirely on the resources of each community. In 1966, the Academy of Sciences released a scathing report on deficiencies in emergency care. According to the report, the average American "had a greater chance of survival in the

Call to Rescue, Call to Heal

Many tools that ambulance attendants use today, such as helicopters, IV's and stretchers, were actually first used in battlefield situations during the Korean and Vietnam wars.

combat zones of Korea or Vietnam than on the nation's highways." It was now obvious to the nation's lawmakers "that trauma . . . [was] a new disease that was primarily taking the lives of young Americans under age 40."

This new awareness stimulated Congress to pass the Highway Safety Act in 1966, which established the Emergency Medical Services (EMS) program. EMS was designed as a community-based program that provides on-the-scene care and transportation for the sick and injured. No longer were emergency crews comprised of doctors dispatched from a hospital or local firefighters. People would be trained specifically to treat medical emergencies outside of a hospital.

In the northwest suburbs of Illinois, which lacked a system of emergency care in the 1960s, up to 70 percent of heart attack victims died en route to the hospital. Stanley Zydlo took charge of designing the country's first multicommunity EMS system in Illinois. "If you don't survive the ride to the emergency room,

The Evolution of Emergency Care

the best doctor in the world and all the advanced technology can't help you." On December 1, 1972, nine Illinois towns were officially mobilized as EMS providers. Thirteen minutes after the system went operational, a call came from a woman choking to death in her living room. Her life was saved. By the 1990s, an estimated 80 percent of heart attack victims covered by that EMS system survived the trip to the hospital.

With the birth of EMS, lawmakers recognized that the task of providing pre-hospital care was an important profession deserving recognition and its own set of standards. "Ambulance attendants" passed into history. Now emergency medical technicians and paramedics treated the wounded and sick at the scene, instead of just transporting them to the hospital. The Department of Transportation developed standards for emergency medical care and helped states to upgrade their pre-hospital care. In 1968, AT&T designated 911 as the universal emergency number.

National recognition of the EMT and paramedic continued at a dizzying pace. The National Registry of Emergency Medical Technicians was founded in 1973 to assist local EMS systems and develop and maintain national standards for the burgeoning number of professional and volunteer EMTs and paramedics. In 1973, Congress passed the National Emergency Medical Services Systems Act. Localities could apply for grants if they met 15 key components, including training and manpower. Two years later, the American Medical Association recognized paramedics as an allied health profession. In 1975, the first New York City paramedic units went into service in out of the Bronx Municipal Hospital Center.

The crucial role emergency workers play in pre-hospital care was highlighted by the adoption of "The Star of Life" as their symbol. The symbol's six-point cross represents the six components of the EMS system—detection, reporting, response, on-scene care, care in transit, and transfer to definitive care—and the staff in the center represents medicine and healing.

Today, an ever-growing number of people are becoming

Call to Rescue, Call to Heal

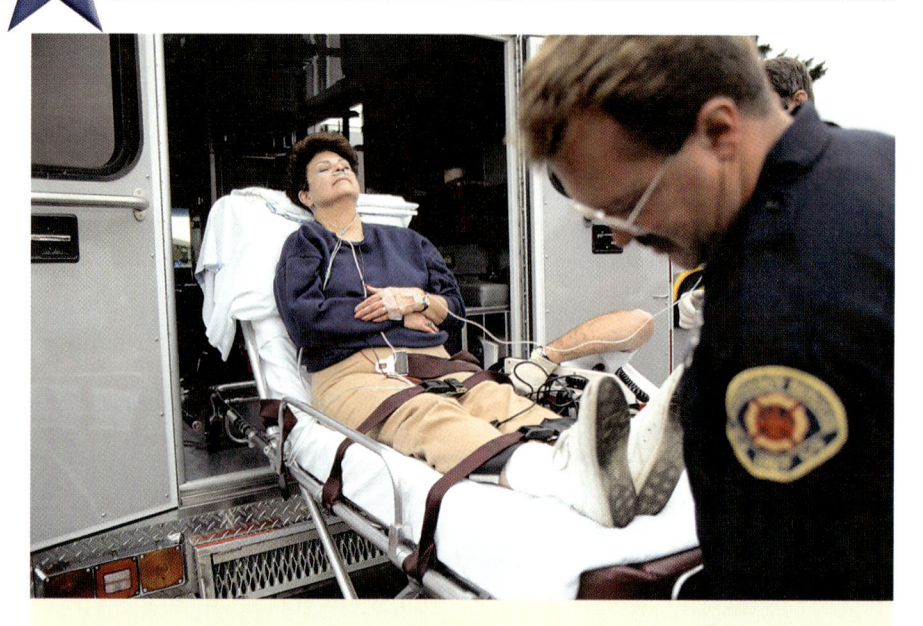

In 1973, the National Registry of Emergency Medical Technicians was founded. This established nationwide standards for EMTs and paramedics, and throughout the '70s, EMTs and paramedics received recognition from Congress and the American Medical Association.

EMTs and paramedics. The Bureau of Labor Statistics reported in 2000 that job demand is expected to grow over the next eight years—partly to keep pace with the aging baby boomer population. In 2000, there were 172,000 EMTs and paramedics. Although there is still a large network of unpaid volunteers nationwide, the trend is that paid professionals will replace volunteers. "People are now looking at it as a profession or career, rather than something to tide them over until they get a 'real job,'" according to a council member with the National Association of Emergency Medical Technicians.

EMTs and paramedics respond to every conceivable medical emergency, from heart attacks, gunshot wounds, and broken bones to attacks from an angry emu. They are also on hand wherever large groups of people are gathered—such as the Olympics, parades and concerts—or wherever there is potential for danger, such as a ski resort or Coast Guard ships. A medic squad

The Evolution of Emergency Care

might also be assigned to the president when he is traveling.

Before the 1960s, providers of emergency care brought whatever skills they happened to have—if any—to the scene of an injury or accident. Today's EMTs and paramedics receive intense training and follow strict guidelines that dictate what they can and cannot do for a patient.

What does it take to become an EMT or paramedic? A potential EMT must be at least 18, possess a high school diploma or GED, and have a valid driver's license. Other qualities—emotional stability, physical strength, dexterity, and calmness—may not be required but are highly recommended. All 50 states and the District of Columbia have an EMS agency that issues licenses to EMTs and paramedics and ensures that its citizens are receiving the best possible emergency care. The process for being licensed combines classes with fieldwork. In addition, most states require students to meet certification requirements outlined by the National Registry of Emergency Medical Technicians (NREMT). Students are trained at colleges, fire academies, hospitals, and technical schools.

Certification, as designated by NREMT, is divided into three categories based on skill level: EMT-Basic, EMT-Intermediate,

EKG (ELECTROCARDIOGRAM)

An EKG records the heart's activity as a series of lines on a moving piece of paper. They show important information about the heart, such as heart rate and rhythm and the presence of current or past heart attacks. An EKG may be given to a patient who is short of breath, lightheaded, or experiencing tightness in the chest. An EKG is given by applying 10 small electrodes to the skin that attached by wire to the EKG machine. On an ambulance, only a paramedic is qualified to interpret an EKG reading.

and EMT-paramedic. There is also a category, known as "first responder," that requires around 40 hours of training. Police and firefighters are typically given first-responder training.

EMT-Basics receive around 110 hours of training. First, they must learn their ABCs: airway, breathing, and circulation. If any of these are compromised, the patient's chance of survival is greatly diminished. EMT-Basics also learn about assessing a patient's condition, administering first aid, giving oxygen, controlling bleeding, delivering babies, and performing cardiopulmonary resuscitation (CPR). EMT-Basics are also skilled in the use of emergency equipment such as backboards and splints. When the extent of injuries goes beyond the EMT-Basic training, the EMT must defer to the next level of EMT or paramedic.

The EMT-Intermediate training requirements differ from state to state and this category is often divided into EMT-II and EMT-III. Generally, they have 200 to 400 hours of training. These EMTs study shock trauma and cardiac arrest. They are trained to administer intravenous fluids and use defibrillators that shock a stopped heart. They can insert IVs, administer a limited number of drugs and obtain blood samples. In certain situations an EMT-Intermediate can perform advanced life support procedures while under instruction from a doctor.

The most advanced level of EMT is the paramedic. Certification as a paramedic involves a two-year program resulting in an associate's degree in applied science. They have 1,000 hours or more of instruction. Paramedics perform advanced life support techniques such as endotracheal intubations, and can administer a variety of drugs, interpret heart-monitoring equipment, and use stomach pumps. Paramedics carry out more complicated procedures under the direction of a doctor via radio.

The salary of EMTs and paramedics is considered one of the drawbacks of the profession. In 2000, the median income for EMTs and paramedics was $22,460. The middle 50 percent earned between $17,930 and $29,270. The lowest 10 percent

The Evolution of Emergency Care

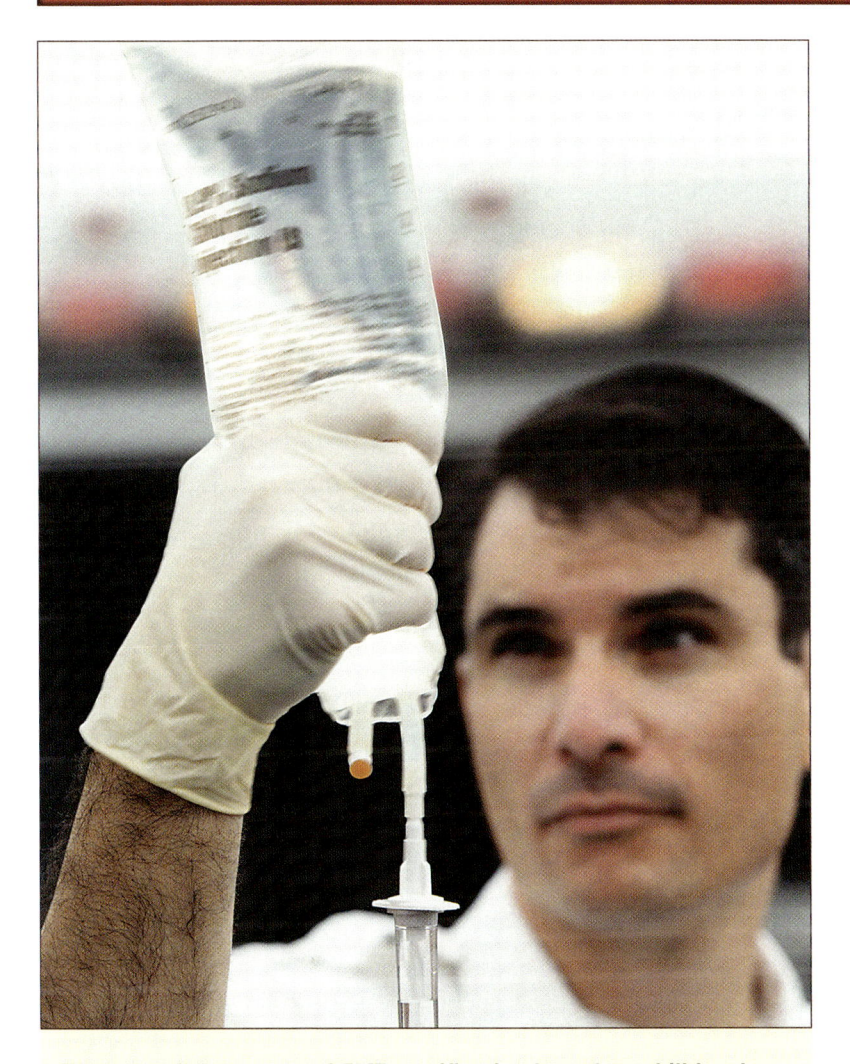

There are three levels of EMT certification based on skill level—EMT-Basic, EMT-Intermediate and EMT-paramedic. EMT-Intermediate training involves skills such as using defibrillators and administering intravenous fluids by inserting IV's.

earned less than $14,660 and the highest 10 percent earned more than $37,760.

The stressful work, plus low pay and long, difficult hours, have contributed to a high turnover rate for emergency medical workers. According to the California Department of Labor, EMTs and paramedics leave the field "mainly due to the unusual work hours and the stress brought on by constantly working in a crisis environment." EMTs and paramedics regularly work 24- to 48-hour shifts, followed by several days off, and can expect to be on call during all major holidays.

Said one veteran paramedic: "There are some systems that are getting paid damn well to do what they do. But we have people within our system who qualify for food stamps and reduced school lunches." On the national level, the National Highway Traffic Safety Administration (NHTSA) oversees EMS. There is no national office or executive agency that manages the nation's EMTs and paramedics. Some EMS veterans continue to lobby for a national office to represent the interests of EMTs and paramedics.

Once an EMT or paramedic is certified they can choose to work as a paid or volunteer EMT. Volunteer and paid EMTs are found in fire stations, hospitals, a county- or government-based service, a private ambulance service or some combination of the above. Volunteer EMTs and paramedics are more commonly found in rural settings. In Fargo, Oklahoma, two farm wives became the volunteer first-responders for tiny Ellis County. With a foot locker of mostly donated equipment, the two women ride to car wrecks, agricultural accidents and heart attacks to stabilize the patient until an ambulance arrives. Two first-responder EMTs in rural Texas started their ambulance service in a double-wide trailer. Their emergency vehicle consisted of an old utility truck with no heat, no air conditioner and holes in the floor. In this instance, a dedication to helping others overcame financial restrictions.

Beyond the mandatory skills EMTs and paramedics must acquire, there are certain environments or fields that require more specialized training. EMTs and paramedics can be found in the wilderness or forest and in the air. An air medic, for instance, does not respond to normal 911 calls. Typically they respond to accidents with mass casualties or extremely life-threatening injuries, when speed is of the absolute essence. Air

The Evolution of Emergency Care

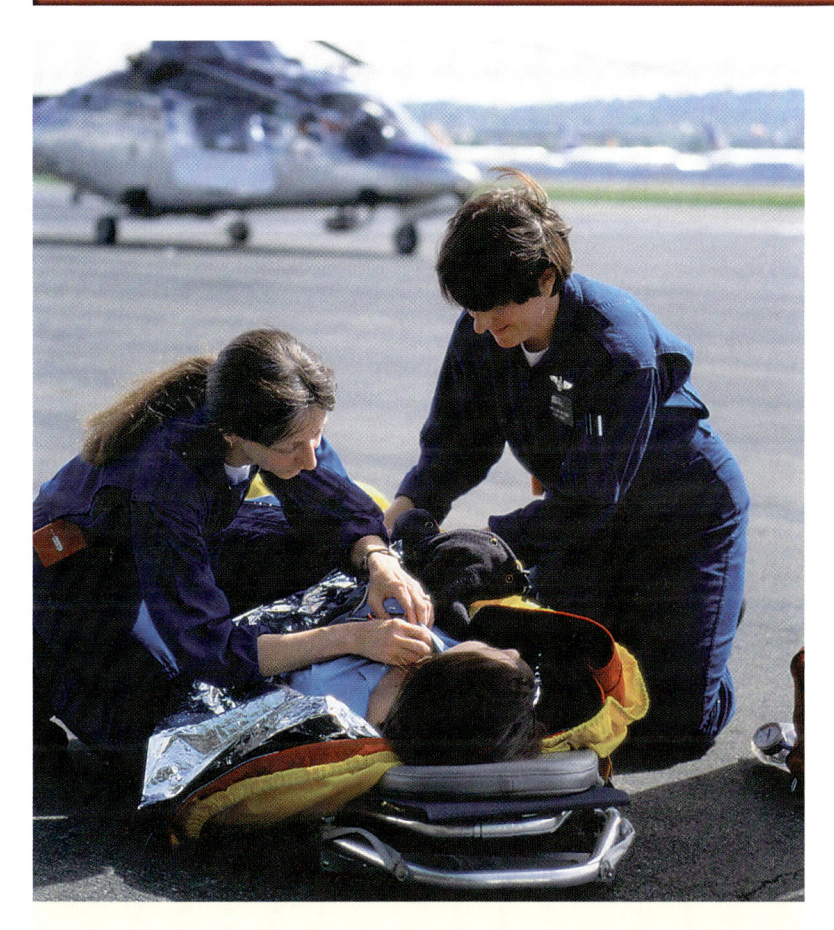

31

Air medics are specialized in dealing with accidents involving mass casualties or extremely life-threatening injuries, as well as transferring patients between hospitals via helicopter.

medics also transfer patients between hospitals. A wilderness EMT is trained to help people suffering from hiking or hunting accidents, including mountain and cave rescue. When the terrain is too steep for an ambulance, the EMT or paramedic must carry up to 40 pounds of equipment to reach the patient. They are also prepared for snow or avalanche conditions that could endanger their lives as well as the patient's. "The biggest challenge we face here [is] having the right equipment for the job and getting it to the patient," said Leslie Terrell, a wilderness paramedic in Oregon.

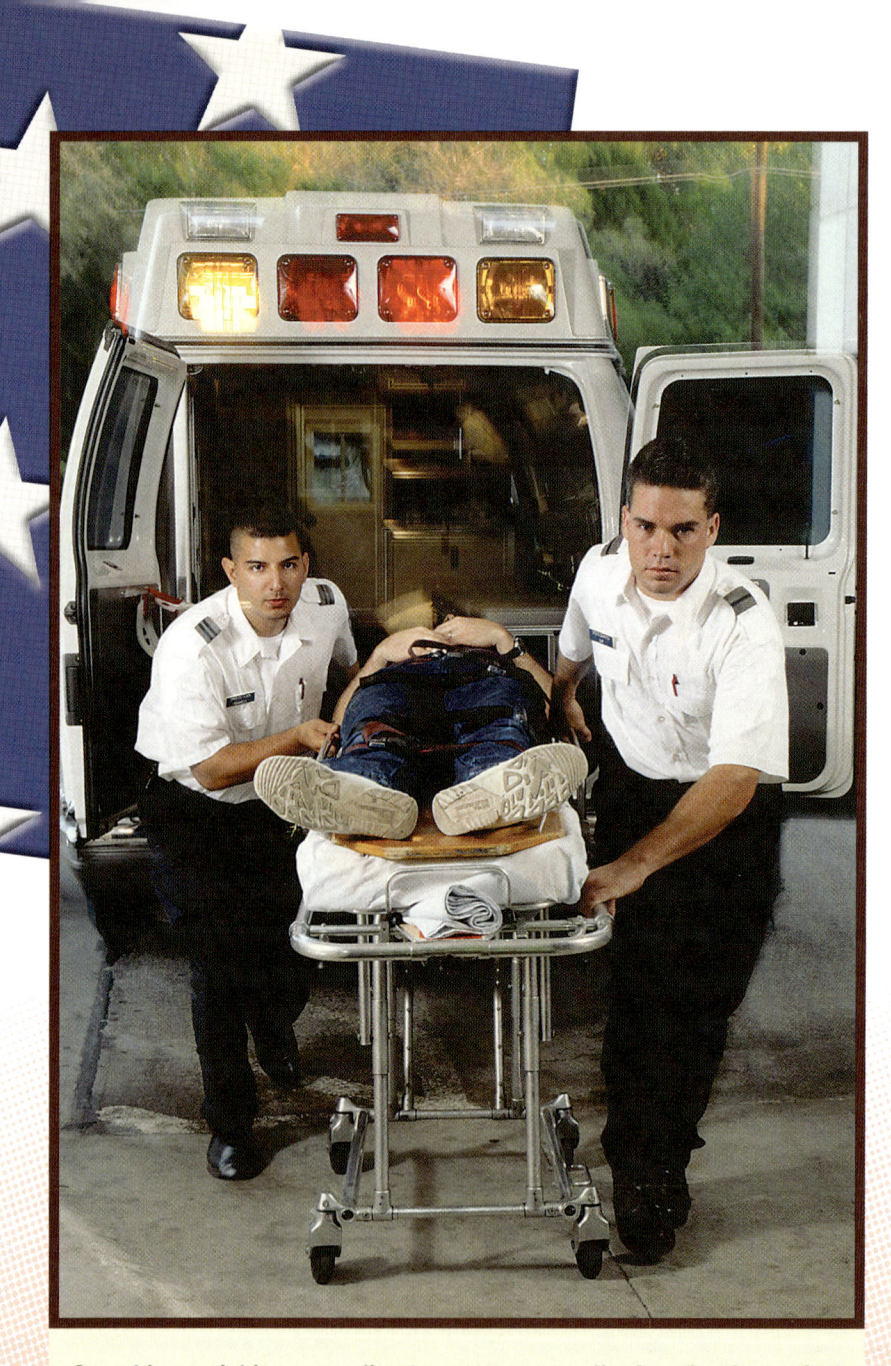

Speed is crucial in responding to emergency calls. A patient's survival rate is highest within the first hour after the injury, so it is crucial that the 911 dispatcher have all the relevant information regarding the patient's injuries and location for the responding ambulance to quickly arrive on the scene and administer care.

3

The Golden Hour and Beyond

For most people, there is nothing golden about that first hour following a heart attack, a severe burn, or a car accident. To EMTs and paramedics, however, the "golden hour" refers to their short window of opportunity to stabilize a critically injured person. If they can give their patient quality treatment within the first hour, the person's chance of survival is, at best, 80 percent. When the golden hour is up, survival rates plunges dramatically to 20 percent after an hour and a half and to one percent at three hours. For children, that crucial time frame is reduced to the "platinum half-hour."

The "golden hour" starts ticking when a dispatcher with a hospital, a police or fire station, or a private ambulance service answers a 911 call. The dispatcher takes a description of what has happened and where it is happening. They also ask a prepared series of questions designed to provide the maximum amount of information to the responding ambulance. When the dispatcher has enough information, they call for an ambulance to respond to the scene. To assist the emergency care providers, most dispatchers have sophisticated computers that map locations and direct ambulances to scene using the quickest route.

The ambulances come from a variety of sources: private services, hospitals, and fire stations are the most common. The ambulance will either be staffed by paid paramedics and EMTs or volunteers. In some communities, firefighters with EMT training respond to emergency medical calls. Other areas rely on ambulances staffed only by paramedics. These are known as Advanced Life Support (ALS) systems because only paramedics have advanced life support training. Other areas rely on a tiered system where all ambulances are staffed by EMTs but not every ambulance has a paramedic. In these systems, it is up to the dispatcher to determine whether the injuries are minimal enough—a broken leg, for instance—to require an EMT or a more severe injury (gunshot wound) that requires paramedic skills.

EMTs and paramedics follow very strict guidelines for what they can and cannot do for a patient. Once they have stabilized a patient, they call a hospital to let them know they are en route. In cases where the patient is critically ill, the ambulance staff might establish contact with a physician via radio who can provide instructions, such as what medications to administer. Sometimes, when the patient is not critically ill, an EMT or paramedic will defer to a doctor instead of giving the patient unnecessary treatment. When a patient is unconscious, EMTs and paramedics must know how to "read" a scene to tell them what has happened.

In all instances, EMTs and paramedics are expected to remain calm. In many cases they must elicit sensitive information from a patient, and a sympathetic tone can calm the patient into talking. And if the patient or family member sees the EMT or paramedic tense or emotional, that can

The Golden Hour and Beyond

add to his or her own sense of panic.

In one example of a 911 call, a 60-year-old woman with a history of asthma is having trouble breathing. Once the call has been dispatched, the nearest ambulance responds to the scene. At the woman's home, the responding EMT takes the woman's pulse and gives her oxygen. The paramedic asks for her medical history, including any medication she is taking. The woman is still having difficulty breathing, so the EMT and paramedic load her onto a stretcher and into the ambulance. The EMT, who will most likely be the driver, calls the nearest hospital to let them know that they are en route and the condition of the patient. On the way to the hospital the woman goes into cardiac arrest. The paramedic begins advanced life support techniques that might include intubation (a tube placed down the throat to keep an airway open) or administering drugs. The EMT will call the hospital again with an update of the woman's condition. When they arrive at the hospital, the EMT and paramedic rush the woman into the emergency room, providing her vital signs and any other important information to hospital staff.

Their job done, the senior emergency worker fills out an incident report. This is an important step. The report is a

DEFIBRILLATOR

A defibrillator restores normal heart rhythm be delivering an electric shock to the heart when the heartbeat has become so fast that the patient risks cardiac arrest. Manual paddles applied to the chest deliver the electrical jolt. The person's heart activity can then be reviewed on an EKG. On an ambulance, only a paramedic can operate a debrillator.

EMTs and paramedics are in constant contact with the nearest hospital in informing them that the ambulance is en route, updating the staff on the patient's status, and in some cases, communicating with a physician who might advise on what medications to administer.

highly detailed account of the emergency response, starting with the time the run began, the ambulance's license number, the location of the call, and the odometer reading. It must also include all of the patient's vital signs, what drugs, if any, were given and how they were administered, the patient's history, allergies, symptoms, skin color, and what treatments were given and how the patient responded. The purpose of the report is two-fold. First, it provides the hospital record of the patient's condition. Second, if the woman dies and her family sued the ambulance service, the report would be an important part of the EMT and paramedic's defense.

After every hospital run, the ambulance is restocked and equipment is sterilized. If the patient had a contagious disease, the crew decontaminates the ambulance. When the ambulance returns to its station every part of the vehicle—gas, oil, battery, sirens, brakes, and radio—are checked to make sure they are working properly.

That's just one example of what might happen on an ambulance run. The daily "routine" of an EMT and paramedic is

The Golden Hour and Beyond

often a million miles away from any definition of routine. "It's something different every day. If you want a scheduled day, don't even plan on [becoming a paramedic]," said Susie Adams, a California paramedic.

The number of runs EMTs and paramedics make each varies widely, depending on their location and local resources. In New York City, members of the Fire Department's Emergency Medical Services respond to more than 1.3 million calls each year. A rural EMS provider might have one call a day. In urban areas, rush hour means an increase in calls due to traffic accidents.

Regardless of where they practice their skills, EMTs and rescue workers be prepared at all times. To ensure their skills stay razor-sharp, EMTs and paramedics must be recertified every two years. If they are at a hospital or fire station, their downtime will likely include some ongoing training. EMTs and paramedics in New York City, for instance, are expected to participate in defibrillator drills every 45 to 90 days. On a slow day, a team of EMT-Bs might re-enact a car accident. Half the team will be the accident victims while the other half prepares splints and stretchers and goes over the questions they must ask. On the walls of fire station or hospital, a list of classes is likely to be posted. The classes are not just for EMTs and paramedics being recertified. They are also for EMT-Bs studying to be EMT-Is, or for EMT-Is studying to become paramedics. With medical care constantly being upgraded, the education of an EMT and paramedic is never complete. "It's a never-ending job trying to keep up," said Dave Witken said. "Medicine is changing drastically, and there are new ways to do things all the time."

The long, emotionally and physically demanding hours EMTs and paramedics work means that teamwork and camaraderie among ambulance partners is very important. Paramedic Al Tregoning recounted to the *Chicago Tribune* how he and his partner rehearse en route to an emergency how they will handle the situation, including the medical protocols and other

Call to Rescue, Call to Heal

EMTs and paramedics must be prepared at all times to deal with a wide range of situations—not only emergencies such as car accidents or fires, but even domestic violence situations.

variables that might affect their ability to provide top-notch care. Constant planning keeps the paramedic and EMT in a prepared state of mind, ready for whatever happens. In addition, it allows partners to know their roles ahead of time. "When you've worked with the same partner for a while, you really know each other's strengths and weaknesses. You don't have to anticipate what he'll do. You know what he'll do," said Mike Schomer, one of Tregoning's partners.

Community service is another important way EMTs and paramedics help out. Their services can empower members of the community to live safely and well before they find themselves riding in the back of an ambulance. Their services often reflect the needs of their community. If there is a large elderly population, health seminars are important. If it's a seaside community, teaching people how to swim safely could reduce the number of drowning. "I don't mean to minimize the importance of running calls—that's why we're here," said Hank Christen, director of emergency management for Okaloosa County, Florida. "But we try to do more than just respond to emergencies as part of our business."

Volunteer rescue squads, which often have tight resources, also provide invaluable non-emergency services. The Northfield Rescue Squad of New Jersey stands by at local school functions and sporting events. Understanding the safety awareness must be ingrained as early as possible, the squad visits schools to explain how 911 works, what a Heimlich maneuver is, and about CPR. Neighboring squads get the benefit of Northfield's generosity as well. "I send out letters to other rescue squads in the area to tell them about our classes and drills and invite them to participate," said Richard Collinson, chief of the Northfield squad. "It's good for everyone."

C-SPINE COLLARS

Protecting the spine from injury is crucial after an accident. EMTs and paramedics place a c-spine collar, a tight-fitting device that runs from the chin to the shoulders, around the neck to prevent the patient from moving it, which limits further spinal injuries.

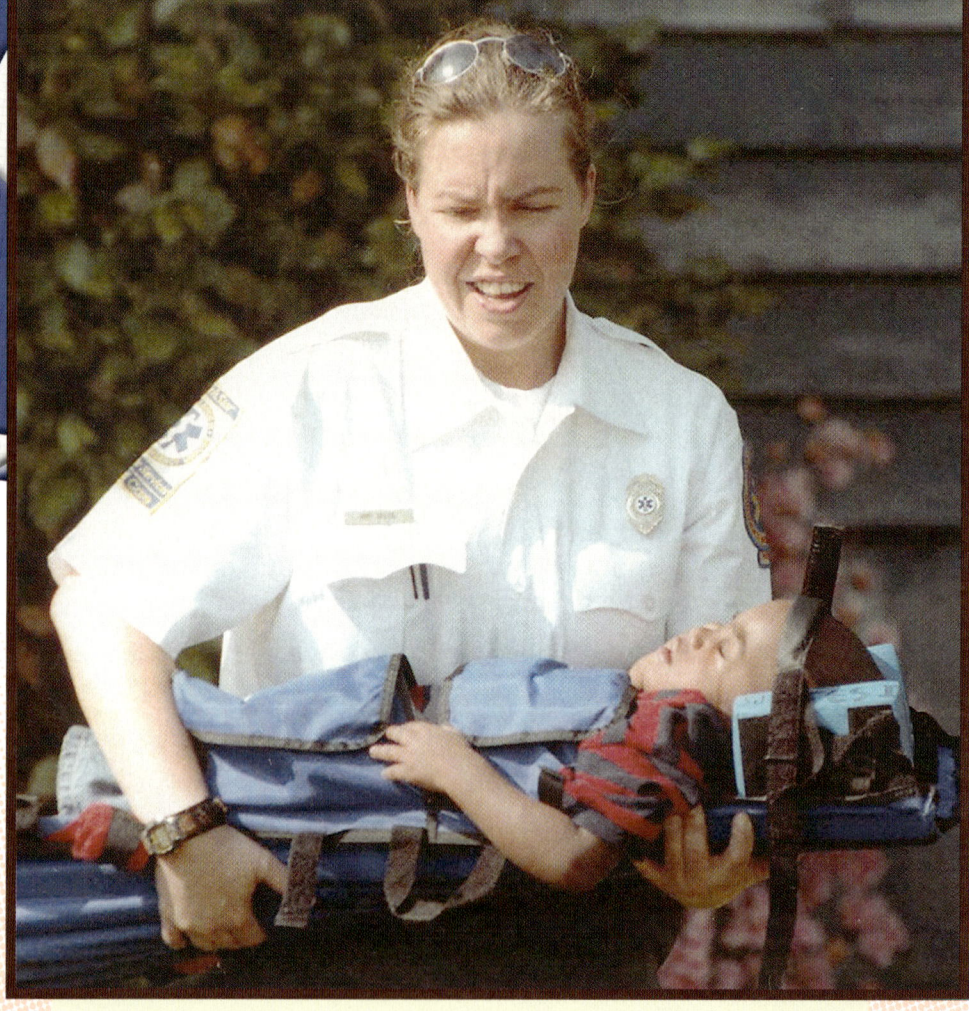

Emergency workers face risks themselves when on the job—from contracting diseases from the patients themselves, violence and threats of bodily harm, or post-traumatic stress syndrome from the emotional strain.

4

Just Part of the Job

EMTs and Paramedics at Risk

A ny profession that involves protecting the public is going to have risks. EMTs and paramedics are under tremendous pressure to reach 911 callers within a certain period of time and to transport them to a hospital as quickly as possible. Physical strength, staying calm in dangerous situations, comforting distraught patients and family members are also routine aspects of the EMT and paramedic's day. A delay or miscalculation could result in the death of a patient. Anyone who has stopped at a green light to let an ambulance speed through an intersection knows that traffic accidents are another risk EMTs and paramedics frequently encounter.

Most health threats to EMTs and paramedics will come from the sick patients they tend to every day. In 1996, a New York City

EMT had to quit her job after contracting Lyme disease and tuberculosis after treating a homeless patient. A Philadelphia paramedic contracted hepatitis C after she performed mouth-to-mouth resuscitation on a newborn baby pulled from a toilet. A study of Portland emergency medical workers in the late 1980s reported over 4 exposures for every 1,000 calls. Overall, the risk of infection is much lower than it once was. This is due to the precautions EMTs and paramedics take—education, wearing gloves, frequently washing hands, cleaning ambulance after every hospital run. There is no documented case of emergency medical work being infected with HIV on the job. A 2000 study by the Centers for Disease Control found that the risk of transmission for hepatitis is minimal.

Encountering disease is a fairly low risk for EMTs and paramedics, but encountering violence is not. EMTS and paramedics are rarely armed. And the threats EMTs and paramedics encounter on a day-to-day basis usually come from the very people they are trying to help and other bystanders. While aiding a gunshot victim, a Chicago EMT had a gun held to his head because the victim's friend didn't think he was working fast enough. A New York City EMT was stabbed while tending to the victim of a fight. Afterward, city officials offered to buy a bulletproof vest for any EMT that wanted one.

A Chicago paramedic told EMS magazine that violence is an unfortunate reality of the job. "One of the unique things about EMS that a lot of people fail to realize is that many times, we're there before the police. In Chicago, our medics have actually witnessed homicides in progress. I'm sure if you talk to any experienced medic, they will tell you that they've encountered some type of violence in their career," said Don Walsh.

In a study of Chicago's EMS system, Walsh discovered that 92 percent of the paramedics he surveyed "had been assaulted at some point while performing their duties, and that in the

Just Part of the Job

course of a 12-year career, each averaged more than nine assaults." It isn't only urban EMTs and paramedics who face danger. More than 40 percent of the Nebraska EMTs that Walsh surveyed reported that they had been assaulted while working. What were some of the reasons for these high figures? Nebraska has a high percentage of illegal labs manufacturing crystal methamphetamine. In Chicago, a series of attacks on emergency personnel was almost entirely the result of patients under the influence of drugs and alcohol. Dealing with a mentally ill patient can also result in a dangerous situation for the responding EMTs and paramedics. When threatened, EMTs and paramedics are supposed to call police for help. The medic's safety comes first, but most EMTs and paramedics will attempt to calm their patient.

Some communities have developed sophisticated programs that allow medics to reach the injured in dangerous settings. In Washington, a SWAT medic team travels to danger zones where other ambulances would not be allowed. These SWAT medics not only wear bulletproof vests but have training in battlefield medical techniques and are armed with 9mm pistols. When a woman in a standoff with police was shot in the neck, a SWAT medic was able to reach the woman's side in 20 seconds.

Techniques for dealing with day-to-day violence can be learned, but there is little preparation for the trauma and horror of a mass casualty situation. Ron Shields, an Oklahoma City EMT, recalled feeling stunned upon seeing the bombed-out remains of the Alfred P. Murrah building. Shields found a woman, still alive, buried up to her neck in debris. As he struggled to free her, Shields was forced to leave when reports of a second bomb came in. "I didn't want to go. There were some police officers and firefighters who came by and they pretty much forced us to leave. It goes against our training." When Shields returned 20 minutes later, the woman had died.

People like EMTs and paramedics, who are trained to help

Call to Rescue, Call to Heal

Many EMTs and paramedics who assisted in the Oklahoma City bombing of the Alfred P. Murrah Federal Building experienced emotional trauma for years after the event. Today EMTs and paramedics acknowledge the need for counseling for their own benefit, especially in cases as catastrophic as the Oklahoma City bombing or the September 11 attacks.

during a crisis instead of seeking safety, don't always recognize when their stress levels are too high. They often accept the pain and trauma they deal with every day as "just part of the job." But EMTs and paramedics who responded to the bombing of a federal building in Oklahoma City in 1995 experienced emotional pain for years afterward. "Some of them have repressed feelings that occasionally come out, usually as fear that a parent is going to die, and sometimes that fear is so overwhelming that it just incapacitates them," said Oklahoma City Fire Department Chaplain Ted Wilson, an EMT-I.

In Oklahoma City, all emergency workers were required to go to a Critical Incident Stress Management (CISM) program when their shift ended. The Federal Emergency Management Agency (FEMA) offered crisis counselors to the city. Afterward, the city developed "Project Heartland" for employees to reach out for emotional assistance whenever they wanted it. Counselors battled the notion that it wasn't "right" for an EMT or paramedic to feel grief over things they witness on the job. "It's traditionally considered an almost 'macho' thing to express anger, but it's not OK to feel vulnerable or sad, so we stuff those emotions and just express anger . . . it doesn't allow for the natural healing to take place, which is what we need to do when we're emotionally injured," said Ted Wilson. "A lot of people like getting sympathy, but not emergency personnel—they just want to get help and get back to what they consider normal as quickly as possible."

It is important for EMTs and paramedics to be able to assess situations and administer care in an organized manner, no matter how chaotic or traumatic the scene might be. This is especially vital in situations with mass casualties, such as the Oklahoma City bombing, shown above.

5

Serving Through Disaster

When a bomb ripped the Alfred P. Murrah Federal Building in Oklahoma City apart on April 19, 1995, a 21-year-old with EMT training was immediately ready to pitch in. Bill Stauffer, a college student, felt the force of the blast shake his classroom. Wanting to help with the rescue effort, Stauffer went to Red Cross headquarters and was eventually shuttled to a makeshift triage unit. After arrriving at the Murrah building, he spent the rest of the day moving medical supplies, helping survivors onto makeshift beds and bringing body bags to rescuers. The terrible images Stauffer saw that day remain with him, but he wouldn't hesitate to help again. "I feel like I helped contribute a good part," he said. "I like to take advantage of opportunities to help people."

Stauffer's attitude is typical of EMTs and paramedics. They want to help the sick and injured. In some instances, like a serious car crash, they will have to treat several people at once. Quickly assessing who is the most injured and who needs care first is a skill all EMTs and paramedics must have. Less common are those emergencies where EMTs and paramedics respond to situations with dozens, even hundreds, of victims. Situations can range from school shootings, chemical spills, or a train wrecks, to natural disasters such as hurricanes, floods, or ice storms. When disaster strikes, multiple ambulances will report to the scene, even if they haven't been called or the emergency is out of their jurisdiction. For example, when EMTs in the West Metro Fire District received word that a shooting was unfolding at Columbine High School, they did not hesitate to assist medics in the neighboring Littleton Fire District. In extreme cases, if the resources of local emergency rescue crews are greatly strained by a disaster, they can request help from the federal government in the form of disaster medical teams. These teams—which include EMTs and paramedics—offer invaluable relief and experience. They are highly trained and carry a wealth of equipment, including protective suits, antibiotics and antidotes, and air-purifying respirators. The teams, stationed around the U.S., can arrive at a disaster scene within several hours of being dispatched.

Emergency medical workers at the scene of a disaster must have a plan and a coordinated system for organizing their resources. This is known as an incident management system (IMS). Traditionally, the first ambulance crew to arrive becomes the incident commander and triage officer. Incident command is transferred to the highest-ranking officer upon their arrival. During a disaster, resources are likely to be strained and confusion can easily occur. It's up the incident commander and triage officer to set priorities and ensure everyone on the scene knows their role and can communicate with each other.

Serving Through Disaster

EMTs and paramedics also have to deal with natural disasters such as storms or floods. Following the IMS, or incident management system, allows emergency medical workers to efficiently coordinate their efforts and resources.

Triage, from the French word "trier," means to sort. To keep track of patients at large disaster scenes, the injured are often given color-coded tags that indicate whether they need immediate treatment, can survive without immediate treatment, or are expected to die. The injured are moved to triage centers until an ambulance is ready or they can be released.

Students flee the premises of Columbine High School. In addition to natural disasters, emergency medical personnel deal with man-made emergencies such as the Columbine shootings, which prevented EMTs and paramedics from reaching patients until the situation had stabilized.

The triage area should be located out of harm's way while still close enough to provide immediate treatment. The challenge of triage lies in grasping a chaotic scene and figuring out an orderly way to care for the injured. Above all, "You do whatever you have to do to stabilize the person," said Dr. Michael Van Rooyen, director of the Johns Hopkins Center for International Emergency Disaster, and Refugee Studies.

Dodging disasters such as floods and hurricanes presents a

Serving Through Disaster

unique set of obstacles. EMTs and paramedics who report to a man-made emergency are also often coming into a highly unstable area. Within hours of responding to the Columbine High School shootings, police were firing over the heads of EMTs and paramedics and SWAT teams were stripping ambulances to use them as shields. No one knew for several hours how many shooters there were and whether they were alive. Bombs kept going off, thwarting rescue efforts. When a paramedic was finally allowed in, he crawled on the ground behind a SWAT team.

When the last of the victims had gone to local hospitals, the first-responding EMTs and medics were able to assess what worked in those chaotic, confusing hours. Jim Olsen said a clearly defined incident management system clarified what everyone's responsibilities were, where they should be, and how they should act. "The scope of this incident was incredible," he said. "Standing against the school and looking back at the staging area, all I could see was rig after rig. I think there were 48 ambulances and EMS crews on the scene. We were fortunate that the incident command system worked well."

The World Trade Center attacks highlighted the importance of emergency medical workers and of the need for special training dealing with other forms of terrorist attacks. Here, EMTs and civilians retreat from the collapsed towers through a sea of dust.

6

Life After September 11

The sheer scope of the attacks on the World Trade Center and the Pentagon sets them apart from any other catastrophe in U.S. history. Police officers, firefighters, EMTs and paramedics saw their ranks painfully shorn within one terror-filled hour. "The EMS community was devastated because we lost almost three times as many people in one day as we'd lost in the last 30 years," said Bob Leonard, a New York City volunteer firefighter and EMT. "In 30 years of EMS as a citywide entity, they lost three people. Never had you looked around and seen eight EMS providers dead in one day. That was a sad day for EMS as a profession."

Rescue workers remained at Ground Zero for days and even weeks after September 11. Many couldn't bear the thought of leaving their fallen comrades behind. "The hardest part was watching the FDNY members work so frantically to find their own," said Terri Boyette, a member of the Ohio Task Force sent to Ground Zero. "They worked nonstop, needing to find something, someone, a ray of hope."

Even for EMTs, paramedics and other rescue workers who have been trained in handling terrorist attacks, watching their worst nightmare come true shook them to the core. Rich Serino, field director of Boston's EMS, said his workers held drills where a small plane or helicopter crashed into the city's Hancock Tower. No one ever imagined they would witness two jetliners crashing into two of the world's tallest buildings. In the days following September 11, Serino wondered if rescue workers would instinctively run into such a dangerous situation again. "You're going to have to look and say, is it safe?"

The tragedy of September 11 will continue to impact EMTs and paramedics in two ways. First, incidents of post-traumatic stress disorder—deep emotional aftershocks experienced after witnessing or suffering through a catastrophic event—have already developed and will likely flare up for years to come. Second, the attacks highlighted the growing awareness that EMTs and paramedics—often the first people on the scene of an emergency—need to receive thorough training for terrorist attacks, including biological and chemical attacks. When a handful of people were infected with anthrax within two months of September 11, it became apparent that EMTs and paramedics would have to recognize the symptoms of biological and chemical terrorism. The anthrax cases and other incidents, such as the sarin gas attack on a Tokyo subway in 1995 that killed 13 people and felled over 5,000 commuters, are few and far between. In October, at the height of the anthrax scare, Boston's EMS received 40 anthrax calls in one day and around 100 calls during the previous week. All of the reports turned out to be harmless substances such as talcum powder, flour, and detergent. Regardless, EMTs and paramedics must be aware of how these deadly agents work. The uneducated EMT

Hazardous materials teams inspect a U.S. Senate building for anthrax decontamination. The anthrax attacks and the many false alarms that followed illustrated the need for EMTs and paramedics to learn how to detect and deal with the effects of biological agents.

and paramedic risks becoming a victim. An educated EMT and paramedic can share their knowledge, which is central to calming anxieties in their community.

"The problem . . . is the external threats that result in them becoming part of the patient load because they don't recognize what's going on," Maniscalco said. There's no doubt that if a biological or chemical attack were to occur, the role of EMTs and paramedics would be in early detection. To that end, in 1996 Congress passed the Defense Against Weapons of Mass Destruction Act. The act provides training, exercises and expert advice to emergency response personnel in 150 U.S. cities. Cities are also eligible for grants to fund personal protective equipment and detection and monitoring devices.

In Louisville, Kentucky—one of the cities chosen for training—emergency personnel learned the finer points of a biological attack that initially appeared to be a fast-moving flu. They were taught to respond cautiously and defensively if an unknown illness began leveling people at a shopping mall. Emergency workers also learned how to wear protective gear and set up decontamination showers. After several months of training, the emergency community—EMS, police, fire, and hospitals—act out a terrorist scenario that tests the techniques and skills they've learned.

Since September 11, the awareness that first-responders require anti-terrorist training and tools has only magnified. New technology is keeping pace with the sophisticated needs of emergency workers. Tools like the small, hand-held sensor that identifies a biological or chemical agent, such as smallpox or chlorine, are in the works.

How else training for EMTs and paramedics will evolve is an ongoing matter of debate. There is not yet a national curriculum for what EMTs and paramedics are taught; variations exist state to state. Not all communities prepare their emergency workers for terrorist attacks. National EMT and paramedics groups suggest that developing federal education standards—that include anti-terrorist training—would be the best way to ensure that all communities are ready and prepared for terrorist attacks. One EMT suggested that the scope of the World Trade Center and Pentagon attacks and continued threats to American security would force communities that hadn't had emergency plans to develop them. "We're slowly reacting as the problem gets more significant," said Hank Christian, an EMT and director of EMS Services for Okaloosa County, FL. "Five years ago, if I'd said that school shooting would be a problem, I wouldn't have been taken seriously; now we have major plans for responding to school shootings."

Drills, practice scenarios and careful plans may avert future disasters, but nothing can lessen the sorrow of those who lost

Life After September 11

EMTs attend to an injured man outside the Beth Israel Medical Center in New York on September 11, 2001. National EMT and paramedics groups are contemplating including anti-terrorist training in future federal education standards for emegency medical workers.

comrades and loved ones on September 11. It is expected that many of those involved in the rescue efforts on that day will suffer from post-traumatic stress disorder. The impact of post-traumatic stress is often devastating. After the Oklahoma City bombing, a study on rescue workers found that 11 committed suicide and police divorce rates skyrocketed by 300 percent.

A person with post-traumatic stress isn't just affected when they are in a stressful situation; often they will panic even when they are in a safe environment. In Brian Gordon's case, not long after September 11 he was outside smoking a cigarette when a plane flew overhead. The EMT immediately dove for cover.

Survivors also struggle with feelings of guilt. Alex Loutsky, the EMT who made the first call when Flight 11 hit the North Tower, said the memories of that tragic day could not to be shaken. "The first few days and a couple of weeks I was running ragged. I felt so grateful to be alive, but I was so guilty to be alive, too," he said. "That was a harrowing time."

For those on the front lines, continuing with what they know best—helping the sick and injured—is the way forward. A poll taken by *EMS Magazine* asked EMTs and paramedics if they felt differently about their job since September 11. Just 2.4 percent said they wanted to leave the field. 51 percent said they felt better about their job, 28 percent said the incident had no effect on their job and 17 percent said they had second thoughts about their careers but chose to stay in the field.

Three months after September 11, 49 new EMTs and nine paramedics joined the ranks of the New York Fire Department. The father of one of the graduates said September 11 had given him a new appreciation for the importance of his son's new job. "With the events lately, it's most important having good people doing these things," said Jim Burbridge. "You understand the importance of the Fire Department and have more appreciation for them."

As Brian Smith suggested, the enormous loss on September 11 will be incomprehensible for a long time. Keith Fairben's father,

CPR

CPR, or cardiopulmonary resuscitation, is an emergency technique applied to someone who has stopped breathing. It is a basic but highly important skill for EMTs and paramedics. The three principles of CPR are known as the ABCs: airway, breathing, circulation. The EMT or paramedic performing CPR provides short breaths into the patient's mouth followed by rapid compressions on the heart to start it beating again. The medic then checks the pulse or listens for breathing and repeats CPR until the person is breathing or a defibrillator is available.

Life After September 11

Dealing with the losses of fellow emergency workers and the sheer trauma of the attacks, EMTs and paramedics comfort each other at a ceremony at Ground Zero held on October 4, 2001. Despite the hardships that came with the September 11 attacks, a survey of EMTs found that only 2.4 percent wanted to leave the field, and that 51 percent actually felt better about their job.

Ken, spent a day digging in the rubble, hoping to bring his EMT son home. He did not find him. Ken Fairben found some solace in knowing his son died taking care of others. "I know that when they find him, he will be with someone. He wouldn't abandon anyone," Fairben said. "I know that he wouldn't have wanted to be anywhere else."

Other survivors echoed Fairben's sentiment. They know EMT and paramedics see their commitment to care as a sacred duty. Cecilia Lillo referred to her husband Carlos Lillo, the EMT who rushed into World Trade Center to find her, as "my hero." "Because I was in there and he was trying to save me," she said.

WEBSITES

http://www.emsmagazine.com
[EMS Magazine]

http://www.ispub.com
[Internet Journal of Disaster and Research Medicine]

http://www.medic-city.com/
[Medic City]

http://www.jems.com
[Journal of Emergency Medical Services]

http://www.ems-c.org/
[Emergency Medical Services for Children]

http://www.nasemsd.org/
[National Association of State EMS Directors]

http://www.nyfd.com
[New York Fire Department]

http://naemt.org/ttrescue/
[To the Rescue Museum]

http://stats.bls.gov/oco/ocos101.htm
[Occupational Outlook Handbook]

http://www.rescue70/org/history.htm
[Mountain Ambulance Service]

ORGANIZATIONS AND AGENCIES

The National Registry of Emergency Medical Technicians
Rocco V. Morando Building
6610 Busch Blvd.
P.O. Box 29233
Columbus, OH 43229
http://www.nremt.org

The National Association of Emergency Medical Technicians
408 Monroe Street
Clinton, MS 39056-4210
http://www.naemt.org

National Highway Traffic Safety Administration
400 7th St. SW
Washington, DC 20590
http://www.nhtsa.dot.gov

FURTHER READING

Canning, Peter. *Rescue 471: A Paramedic's Stories*. New York: Ballantine Books, 2000.

Canning, Peter. *Paramedic: On the Front Lines of Medicine*. New York: Ivy Books, 1998.

Tangherlini, Timothy R. *Talking Trauma: Paramedics and Their Stories*. Jackson: University Press of Mississippi, 1998.

Thiesen, Donna and Dary Matera. *Angels of Emergency: Rescue Stories from America's Paramedics and EMTs*. Lincoln: *iUniverse.com*, 2000.

BIBLIOGRAPHY

Adler, Jerry. "After the Attack." *Newsweek*, September 24, 2001.
Aiken, Charlotte. "Training Can't Make Workers Immune." *The Daily Oklahoman*, July 30, 1995.
Anderson, Charles. "Patient-Care Documentation." *EMS Magazine*, March 1999.
Baker, Al. "Grief for Fallen Rescuers, But It's Just the Beginning." *New York Times*, September 15, 2001.
Barry, Dan. "Pictures of Medical Readiness, Waiting and Hoping for Survivors." *New York Times*, September 12, 2001.
"Becoming an EMT: What Does It Take?" *LearnATest.com*.
    http://www.learnatest.com/ems/careeradvice/careerright2.cfm
Boyette, Terri. "Return to Normal Life After WTC." *EMS Magazine*, December 2001/January 2002.
Bragg, Rick. "Events of Day Return as Ghosts in the Night." *New York Times*, September 14, 2001.
Branton, John."Team Brings Medicine Into the Line of Fire." *The Columbian*, December 27, 2001.
Breslau, Karen. "Reporting on United Flight 93." *Newsweek*, November 26, 2001.
Buckley, Jerry. "The Shame of Emergency Care for Kids." *U.S. News and World Report*, January 27, 1992.
Caldwell, Andrew. "Critical Incident Stress: The Pain in the Aftermath." *EMS Magazine,* 2001.
California Occupational Guide Number 550. California Employment Development Department.
Circle Safety & Health Consultants. "Protecting the EMS Care Giver: A Study of Work Place Violence Risks & Controls Within the Emergency Medical System of Virginia." Virginia Department of Health, Office of Emergency Medical Services.
Cooper, Glenda. "A Muslim Family in N.Y. Fears for a Son Who Loved America." *Washington Post*, September 18, 2001.
Cromley, Allen. "Preparedness Paid Off on April 19, Paramedics Say." *The Daily Oklahoman*, July 13, 1995.
Daly, Michael. "Second-By-Second Terror Revealed in Calls to 911." *New York Daily News*, September 30, 2001.
Davis, Kirsten. "Paramedic Partners Buried While Saving Lives." *New York Post*, September 21, 2001.
"Domestic Terrorism: Issues of Preparedness." National Association of State Emergency Medical Services Directors, 2001.
Drick, Joe. "Riverboat EMS: Never a Game of Chance." *EMS Magazine*, March 1998.
Due, Tananarive. "Turbulence Remains For Kids Who Weathered the '92 Storm." *Miami Herald*, August 21, 1994.
"Emergency Medical Technician Job Descriptions." *LearnATest.com*.
    http://www.learnatest.com/ems/careeradvice/jobopp2.cfm
"EMS Education Agenda for the Future: A Systems Approach." National Highway Traffic Safety Administration, June 2000.
"EMS History." FDNY website. *http://www.ci.nyc.ny.us/html/fdny/html/ems_week/ems_history.html*
"EMS History." Wyoming Office of Emergency Medical Services.
Erich, John. "From Provider to Patient: Injured in the Line of Duty." *EMS Magazine*, March 2001.
Erich, John. "Howling At The Moon: Violent Patients Taking It Out on EMS." *EMS Magazine*, October 2001.
Erich, John. "Life on Alert: Nation Remains Jittery as Threats Keep Coming." *EMS Magazine*, November 2001.
Erich, John. "The State of EMS." *EMS Magazine*, April 2001.
Erich, John. "Wheels of Fortune." *EMS Magazine*, November 2000.
Etter, Jim. "Fargo Farm Wives Try Hand as EMTs." *The Daily Oklahoman*, June 3, 1991.
Fimrite, Peter and Nolte, Carl. "Storm Surges, Mud Slides." *San Francisco Gate*, December 11, 1996.
Finder, Alan. "Ambulance Service is Faster, But Medical Gains Are In Doubt." *New York Times*, April 26, 1999.
France, David, Gates, David, and McGuigan, Cathleen. "The Spirit of America." *Newsweek*, September 27, 2001.
Freeman, Calvin, Iabell, Darlene, Morales, Joseph, and Smiley, Daniel. "Medical Care for the Injured: The Emergency Care Response to the April 1992 L.A. Civil Disturbance." Doheny Electronic Resources Center at the University of Southern California.
Gelzinis, Peter. "Attack on America: Horror Beyond Imagining Has Become Too Real." *Boston Herald*, September 14, 2001.
Gest, Emily. "8 EMS Heroes Killed at WTC Remembered." *New York Daily News*, November 19, 2001.

BIBLIOGRAPHY

Glarum, Jan. "Tactical EMS." Oregon Public Health Services.

Godfrey, Ed. "City is Helm of Hurricane Disaster Aid." *The Daily Oklahoman*, August 25, 1992.

Graham, Jessie, Haberman, Maggie, and Mangan, Dan. "Heroes Emerge Amid Chaos." *New York Post*, September 12, 2001.

Graham, Judith. "Small Communities Plan For Terror Threat; Areas Lack Trained Emergency Staffs." *Chicago Tribune*, October 22, 2001.

Grosscup, Luann. "For Shore Search and Rescue, Immigrant Interventions, Storm Assistance All in a Day's Work for the Coast Guard." *Chicago Tribune*, January 10, 1999.

Hanchar, J. "Bearing Witness: Responders Tell Their Stories." *Journal of Emergency Services*, October 2001.

Hansen, Jane. "Tech at Forefront of Detection." *The Atlanta Journal-Constitution*, October 11, 2001.

"Hepatitis C Virus Infection Among Firefighters, Emergency Medical Technicians, and Paramedics, Selected Locations, United States, 1991-2000." *MMWR Weekly*, July 28, 2000.

"History and Meaning of the Star of Life." National Association for Emergency Medical Technicians Online. http://www.naemt.org/star.htm

"History of the Mountain Ambulance Service." The Mountain Ambulance Service.

"History of Volunteer Rescue and EMS Today." National Association of Emergency Medical Technicians Online/To The Rescue Museum. http://naemt.org/ttrescue

Hopper, Leigh. "Neighbors Are the Lifeblood of Outlying EMS: Volunteer Ambulance Services are Difference Between Life, Death." *Austin American-Stateman*, October 7, 1996.

Hulse, Carl. "Readying Emergency Teams for Terrorist Attacks." *New York Times*, July 3, 1999.

Ibarguen, Diego. "Paramedic Who Lost Ambulance at Trade Center September 11 Accepts Donation for New Vehicle." Associated Press, December 14, 2001.

Jackson, Mike. "Paramedic's Work is Varied and Tough." *St. Petersburg Times*, October 17, 1992.

Klinka, Karen. "Medi Flight Air Ambulance Saves Time, Oklahomans' Lives." *The Daily Oklahoman*, December 27, 1992.

"Learn About EMS." National Registry of Emergency Medical Technicians.

Ledford, Joey. "Traffic Death More Likely if Wreck Is in Rural Area." *The Atlanta Journal-Constitution*, January 23, 2002.

Loft, Kurt. "Survivors Cope with Problems of Life After Storm 5." *The Tampa Tribune*, August 27, 1992.

Love, Bernie. "Paramedic Learns to Stay Cool in a Crisis." *The Daily Oklahoman*, March 4, 1990.

Mandernach, Mark. "'People Shouldn't Die.'" *Chicago Tribune*, June 12, 1994.

"Mayor Giuliani and Fire Commissioner Von Essen Honor Hero Paramedics and Emergency Medical Technicians at EMS Medal Day." Archives of the Mayor's Press Office (New York City), February 18, 1998.

Mbugua, Martin. "Terrorist Attack Haunts Medic." *New York Daily News*, December 15, 2001.

McPhee, Michele and O'Shaughnessy, Patrice. "The Great Rescue of September 11: How Heroes Saved Countless Lives When Terror Struck." *New York Daily News*, November 11, 2001.

Moore, Elizabeth. "America's Ordeal: Dreams on Replay." *Newsday*, October 28, 2001.

Morrello, Carol. "Va. EMT Among Missing in N.Y." *Washington Post*, September 19, 2001.

"Most Stressful Jobs." *Miami Herald*, October 26, 1997.

Murphy, William. "Terror Attacks: Scrambling to Safety Was a Gamble." *Newsday*, September 18, 2001.

Nordberg, Marie. "The Cream of the Crop." *EMS Magazine*, May 1999.

Nordberg, Marie. "Emergency Medical Dispatch: A Changing Profession." *EMS Magazine*, August 1998.

Nordberg, Marie. "Is EMS Ready for Domestic Terrorism?" *EMS Magazine*, April 2000.

Nordberg, Marie. "Oklahoma City Remembers." *EMS Magazine*, April 2000.

Nordberg, Marie. "When Kids Kill: Columbine High School Shooting." *EMS Magazine*, October 1999.

O'Shaughnessy, Patrice. "Terror Attacks Take Hidden Toll." *New York Daily News*, January 20, 2002.

Occupational Outlook Handbook. U.S. Department of Labor.

Okie, Susan and Brown, David. "Response Centers Mobilize to Provide Care for Injured." *Washington Post*, September 12, 2001.

Photo caption. "Heroes." *New York Post*, September 14, 2001.

Raia, Patrice. "Rescue Crew Honored For Helping Save Blast Victim." *Chicago Tribune*, December 12, 1998.

BIBLIOGRAPHY

Ricks, Delthia. "Street-wise Medical Help Often Vital." *Newsday*, September 13, 2001.

Ross, Jr., Bobby. "Just One Hero Among Many." *The Daily Oklahoman*, April 24, 1995.

Smith, Paul. "Weapons of Mass Destruction: Part I, Chemical Agents." *The Internet Journal of Research & Disaster Medicine*.
http://www.ispub.com/ostia/index.php?xmlFilePath=journals/ijrdm/vol2n1/terror1.xml

Sonnier, Todd. "Emergency Workers Cope with Job Trauma." *Austin American-Statesman*, January 18, 2000.

Spielman, F. "'I Thought I Was Going to Die,' Paramedic Says." *Chicago Sun-Times*, June 19, 2001.

Spivak, Mike. "Trauma Care in EMS: Where Are We?" *EMS Magazine*, April 1999.

Staff report. "Bronx Man Is Convicted of Stabbing Technician." *New York Times*, April 10, 1998.

Staff report. "EMS Poll." EMT City. http://www.emtcity.com

Staff report. "Flirting with Danger on the Slopes." *San Francisco Gate*, January 11, 1998.

Steele, Jeffrey, "A Career On The Move In Emergency Care." *Chicago Tribune*, October 15, 2000.

Streger, Matthew. "Prehospital Triage." *EMS Magazine*, June 1998.

Sulski, Jim. "Veteran EMT Puts Patients First; Life and Death Situations Offer Challenges, Rewards." *Chicago Tribune*, January 28, 1998.

Talan, Jamie. "America's Ordeal: Saving People Was His Passion." *Newsday*, September 20, 2001.

Terrell, Leslie. "Medical Response in the Wilderness Environment." Oregon Department of Human Services.

Twomey, Steve and Arthur Santana. "Terrorists Hijack 4 Airliners, Destroy World Trade Center, Hit Pentagon; Hundreds Dead." *Washington Post*, September 12, 2001.

Virasami, Bryan. "New EMTs Join Fire Department." *Newsday*, December 13, 2001.

Wedge, David and Lawrence, J.M. "War on Terrorism; AG: Pranksters Will Pay; Vows Disease Hoax Will Lead to Hard Time." *Boston Herald*, October 18, 2001.

"What EMS Is and How It Began." Ohio Department of Public Safety.
http://www.state.oh.us/odps/division/ems/data/cat7/emswhat.html

Winter, Christine. "Emergency Response A Science For Fire Chiefs." *Chicago Tribune*, October 18, 1998.

Zelinski, Becky. "Paramedic Real Lifesaver." *The Bakersfield Californian*, February 27, 2002.

Zuckoff, Mitchell. "Reliving the Morning of Death." *The Boston Globe*, September 16, 2001.

PICTURE CREDITS

3: Associated Press, Wide World Photos
8: Associated Press, Wide World Photos
11: Associated Press, Wide World Photos
13: Associated Press, Wide World Photos
15: Associated Press, Wide World Photos
17: Associated Press, Wide World Photos
22: Hulton Archive by Getty Images
24: Associated Press, Wide World Photos
38: Associated Press, Wide World Photos
40: Associated Press, Wide World Photos
44: Associated Press, Wide World Photos
46: Associated Press, Wide World Photos
49: © Bettmann/Corbis
50: © AFP/Corbis
52: Associated Press, Wide World Photos
55: © AFP/Corbis
57: Associated Press, Wide World Photos
59: Associated Press, Wide World Photos

Cover: Associated Press, AP

JENNIFER PELTAK graduated from Temple University with a degree in journalism. She was previously a reporter and editor with two newspapers in northern Virginia. She currently resides in Washington, D.C.

INDEX

Advanced Life Support systems, 34, 35
Air medics, 30-31
Ambulance attendants, 23, 25
Ambulances, 24, 35-37
  history of, 21-22, 23
Anthrax, 54

Bellevue Hospital, 21-22
Biological and chemical attacks, 54-56

Certification, 27-28, 30, 37
Civil War, 21
Columbine High School shootings, 48, 51
Community service, 39

Defense Against Weapons of Mass
  Destruction Act, 55-56
Disaster medical teams, 48
Disasters, 9-17, 43-44, 47-51, 53-59
Dispatchers, 33-34, 35

Emergency medical care, history of, 20-25
Emergency Medical Services (EMS)
  program, 24-25
Emergency medical technicians (EMTs)
  /paramedics
  and disasters, 9-17, 43-44, 47-51, 53-59
  and health threats, 41-42, 54-56
  history of, 24-25
  need for, 26, 58
  number of, 26
  as paid/ or volunteer, 26, 28-29, 30, 34
  requirements for, 27
  and risks, 41-45, 54-57
  routine of, 35-37
  and stress, 43-45, 54, 56-58
  symbol of, 25
  tasks of, 19-20, 26-28, 30, 34-36, 39, 59
  and teamwork, 37-39
  training for, 20, 27-28, 30-31, 37, 55-56
  and treatment in first hour, 33-34
  turnover rate for, 29-30
  and violence, 42-43
  work hours of, 30, 37

Firefighters, and emergency care, 22, 24

Golden hour, 33-34

Highway Safety Act, 24

Hospitals, and emergency pre-hospital
  treatment, 21-22, 23

Incident management system, 48, 51
Incident report, 35-36
International First Aid and Rescue
  Association, 23

Korean War, 23

Larrey, Baron Dominique Jean, 20
License, 27
Lincoln, Abraham, 21

Medics, 22-23, 30-31

Napoleon, 20-21
National Emergency Medical Services
  Systems Act, 25, 30
National Registry of Emergency Medical
  Technicians (NREMT), 25, 27
911, 25, 33, 41

Pentagon. *See* September 11
Police, and emergency care, 22
Post-traumatic stress disorder, 54, 57

Recertification, 37
Red Cross first aid training, 22
Rescue squads, 22-23

September 11 terrorist attacks, 9-17, 53-59
Staging areas, and September 11, 10
"Star of Life, The" (symbol), 25
SWAT medics, 43

Terrorist attacks, 9-17, 43-44, 47, 53-59
Triage officer, 48
Triage stations, 10, 49-50
  history of, 20-21
  and Oklahoma City bombing, 47
  and September 11, 10, 14-15, 16

Volunteer medics, 22-23
Volunteer rescue squads, 39

Wilderness EMTs, 31
Wise, Julian Stanley, 22-23
World Trade Center. *See* September 11
World War II, 23